Can't Never Could

Lesson: Confidence

Written by Jason Adams
and
Illustrated by Hannah Adams

To order additional copies of this book, contact:
Xlibris
1-888-795-4274
www.Xlibris.com
Orders@Xlibris.com

Dedicated to my mother and Karate teachers.

Growing up I saw my mom always try her best. Through her hard work and effort she made great things happen all around her. Her example is what made me who I am today. Thanks Mom.

-Your Loving Son

Zack sat watching the kids play outside. He had never played with them before, but had always wanted to ask to join them. Zack was scared to ask. He was afraid to try and play with kids he had never met before. "Zack, what are you doing and why so sad?" his mother asked. "Nothing," he replied as he looked out the window. "Zack, why don't you go try and ask if they will let you join their game?" said his mom. Zack's mother walked out of his room as he sat there thinking if he should go try and ask, or not.

The next day, Zack and his family drove to the store. On their way there they passed a Karate school which they drove by regularly. "Zack, it's the Karate school you talked about wanting to join," his mother said, "You want to stop and check it out?" "Mom, I don't know Karate you know that," Zack replied. "Well we could always see what it is about and let you try," she told him.

Zack's dad stopped at the Karate school and as they went in Zack became scared. He was afraid he wouldn't be welcomed since he didn't know much about Karate except what he had seen on television. What if he wasn't any good at it? What if the other kids laughed at him or what if he just couldn't do it? All these things went through his mind as they entered.

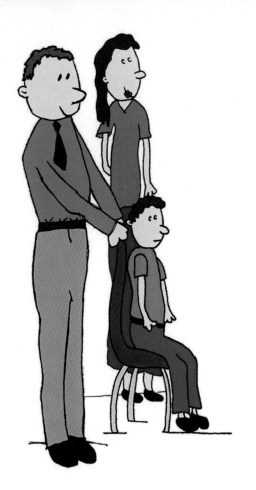

Once they entered the Karate school, Zack sat and watched the class of kids punching. Zack's parents stood watching, but they saw something different. They saw the kids were having fun and knew this was what Zack needed. The kids punched and yelled, which made Zack wonder why were the kids yelling, how did they know what or how to yell. Zack knew if he yelled the other kids would laugh at him since he didn't yell like them. Zack started feeling more scared than when he first walked in, he knew the kids would not accept him.

Zack had not noticed the instructor until now. He listened as the instructor yelled out in a different language he didn't know. Then the kids punched again and yelled. Zack looked and could only say, "I can't do that!" "I don't even know what he said to make them punch," Zack told his parents. The instructor continued to yell out commands, "Ichi, Ni, San…," while the students followed each command with another punch and yell.

While Zack watched, the instructor came over to his parents and him. "Konnichiwa welcome, I am Sensei Cope," the instructor said. He continued talking to Zack, "Would you like to start learning the way of Karate?" Zack could not believe the instructor wanted him to start right then, he didn't even know what the other kids were doing. Scared to move or speak, Zack just sat watching. Then Sensei Cope said to Zack, "you know, why not try it can't hurt".

Sensei Cope asked Zack to come join him. Zack stood looking back at his parents. Sensei Cope then asked, "Well young man, what is your name?" Zack replied, "Uh, Zack." "Well, Zack you can take your socks and shoes off and place them on the shelf. Then join me over here for your first lesson, how to bow," Sensei Cope told him.

After showing Zack how to bow, Sensei Cope showed Zack how to punch and then said to him, "Ok Zack now try punching with me." Zack told Sensei Cope, "I can't do that!" Zack was more worried that he would not be as good as the other students. Zack looked at the other kids kicking and yelling now. One thing Zack noticed was the kids seemed happy and they were having fun. "Don't worry about what you don't know, just be willing to try your best," Sensei Cope told Zack, "now let's work on punching."

Zack followed Sensei Cope's instructions and began to mirror his movements. Sensei Cope went slow as he told Zack, "try again, you're doing very well." They continued several times, each time Sensei Cope would tell Zack, "keep trying, you're getting it."

Zack began getting into his punches and his parents could see he was trying harder. He even forgot about the other students as they kicked and yelled. The more Zack tried punching with Sensei Cope, the more fun he began to have, knowing he was getting better with each try.

Zack's parents were so proud to see their son having fun while trying something new. They knew Zack had learned more than just Karate that night. "Sensei Cope, I can," Zack shouted! Sensei Cope did not have to say a word he just smiled and bowed to Zack as he instructed the students to line up for the end of class.

The students stood in line clapping as Zack was presented his uniform. Even though the other kids had been practicing they saw Zack training with Sensei Cope. Each one remembered their first class and how far they had come since then. The students knew Zack could go just as far, as long as he continued trying. "I am proud to present you with your uniform for your hard work this evening," Sensei Cope told Zack.

Sensei Cope told the students, "I ask that we all welcome Zack and help him along the way, the Way of Karate, as he continues his journey of learning the lessons Karate has to offer." Zack made new friends that night as he stood there in class now like the other students. "Zack, you will learn Karate has much to offer more than just self-defense, but it can teach you self-confidence and more," Sensei Cope said. "Does anyone have any questions," he asked.

"Zack we are so proud of you, you did so well and tried so hard," his mother said. "You looked like a regular Karate kid, good job," Zack's dad told him. "Sayonara, Zack we look forward to seeing you next class. It was an honor having you join our dojo tonight," Sensei Cope said.

That weekend, Zack's mother found her son sitting on his bed sad as she had seen him so many times before. His mother asked, "Zack, why so sad?" Zack replied, "It's nothing." "Zack, you know the kids are playing outside and all you have to do is go ask them if you can try and play," she said to him.

Zack jumped up from his bed and shouted, "You're right, all I have to do is try, thanks mom!" Zack was confident he could try no matter what because he knew now if he tried he could, even if it took more than one try. Zack's mother was happy because she saw that her son had learned a valuable lesson in self-confidence. She told Zack, "Well, go ahead son go play," as she walked out of his room.

As Zack walked up to the kids, one of the girls said, "Hi, we are playing soccer." Zack thought for a minute, I don't know how to play soccer. He then asked, "Can I join even if I don't know how to play?" The boy then said, "Sure we can show you how, its lots of fun." Zack was happy to try and play with them all while having fun.

Try and you can!

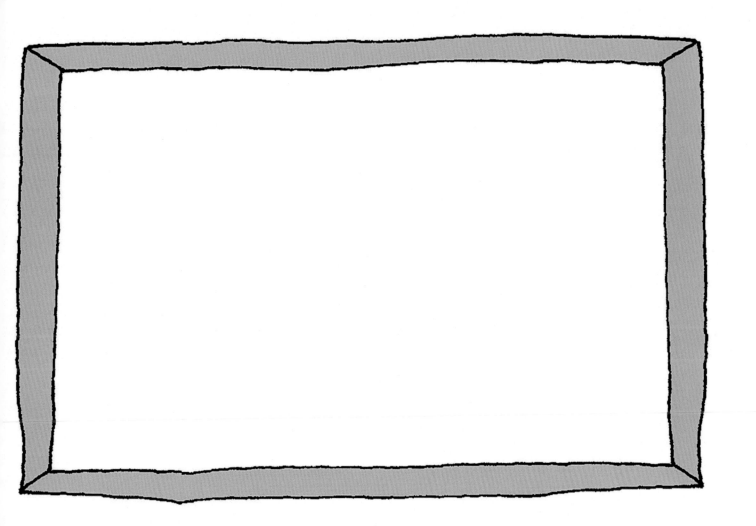

I hope you enjoyed reading about gaining confidence by trying and giving your best. Each time you try, you learn you can and the results are so rewarding. In the space above write or draw something you want to learn to do, but have not tried yet. Now, I hope you reach your goal, but if not just keep trying!

Printed in the United States
By Bookmasters